In the Name of Allah, The All-Merciful,
The Kindest towards believers.

Disclaimer

All rights reserved. No part of this publication may be reproduced, stored in a retrieval system, or transmitted in any form or by any means, electronic, mechanical, photocopying, recording, or otherwise, without the prior written permission of the publisher, except in the case of brief quotations quoted in articles or reviews.

Contact : Admin@islamiclessonsmadeeasy.com.au

Visit us :
Facebook.com/islamiclessonsmadeeasy
Youtube.com/islamiclessonsmadeeasy
Instagram.com/islamic_lessons_me
Islamiclessonsmadeeasy.com.au
Ilme.net.au

The pictures used are the property of Islamic Lessons Made Easy. The content and rulings are taken from various leading scholars and are presented in a simplified manner. Therefore, for the exact definition and explanation, please refer to the original sources.

First Edition
©Copyright 2025 Islamic Lessons Made Easy

Contents

Transliteration	4
Introduction	5
Etiquettes of Qurān	6
Sūrah al-Falaq	8
Summary	24
Glossary	28

Transliteration

ا	a	ق	q
ب	b	ك	k
ت	t	ل	l
ث	th	م	m
ج	j	ن	n
ح	ḥ	ه	h
خ	kh	و	w
د	d	ي	y
ذ	dh	ئ / آ / ـَا	ā
ر	r	ـِي	ī
ز	z	ـُو	ū
س	s		
ش	sh		
ص	ṣ		
ض	ḍ		
ط	ṭ		
ظ	ẓ		
ع	ʿ		
غ	gh		
ف	f		

ء	Read with a sudden pause of air.
ﷺ	Blessings of Allah be upon him and his family.
عليها السلام	Peace be upon her.
عليه السلام	Peace be upon him.
ﷻ	Glorious and Exalted Is He.

Introduction

Tafsīr is an Arabic word that means 'explanation'; it helps us understand what the verses of the Qurān really mean. Scholars study the Qurān by looking at its language, the history behind the verses and other aspects. They also think about how the verses were revealed and how we can use these teachings in our daily lives.

Tafsīr helps us connect with our faith and learn how to use the lessons of the Qurān today. It makes the wisdom of the Qurān easier to understand and more useful for us.

When we made this *Tafsīr*, we worked hard to gather ideas from trusted scholars and important books. We wanted to explain the Qurān in a way that is easy for you to understand.

We hope this *Tafsīr* helps you on your journey to learn more about the Qurān and your faith.

Etiquettes of Qurān

Before reciting, it is recommended to say:

أَعُوذُ بِاللَّهِ مِنَ الشَّيْطَانِ الرَّجِيمِ

Aʿūdhu billāhi minash shayṭānir rajīm

I seek refuge with Allah from the accursed devil.

Then say:

بِسْمِ اللَّهِ الرَّحْمَٰنِ الرَّحِيمِ

Bismillāhir Raḥmānir Raḥīm

In the name of Allah, The Most Gracious, The Most Merciful.

- Make sure you have performed *Wuḍū* before touching any verse of the Qurān
- When reading the Qurān, it is better to face the *Qiblah*
- Make sure that the place where the Qurān is read is free from impurities
- Don't put the Qurān on the ground or anywhere it might get dirty
- Don't place anything on top of the Qurān
- When you recite the Qurān, try to pronounce the words correctly
- Take time to reflect on what the verses mean

After finishing your recitation, say:

صَدَقَ اللهُ العَلِيُّ العَظِيمُ

Ṣadaq Allāhul ʿAliyyul ʿAẓīm

Allah, the Sublime, the Great, has spoken the truth.

Sūrah al-Falaq

Sūrah al-Falaq

Sūrah al-Falaq is the 113th chapter of the Qurān. It is short but powerful, teaching us to ask Allah ﷻ for protection from all types of harm and evil.

Sūrah al-Falaq is often recited with Sūrah al-Nās. Together, they are called the Muʿawwidhatayn (الْمُعَوِّذَتَيْن), meaning "the two chapters of seeking refuge", and are known for protecting believers from harmful influences.

Some reports suggest that Sūrah al-Nās and Sūrah al-Falaq were revealed when a magician cast a spell on the Prophet Muhammad ﷺ, causing him to fall ill.

The angel Gabriel informed the Prophet ﷺ that the spell was hidden in a well, tied in a string with multiple knots. The Prophet ﷺ instructed Imām ʿAlī ؑ to retrieve it. Imām ʿAlī ؑ then untied the knots while reciting the verses of the two Sūrahs, and with each knot untied, the effects of the spell were undone, restoring the Prophet's health.

However, many scholars have dismissed this story, noting that the Qurān clearly indicates that the Prophet ﷺ is protected from the influence of magic and satanic forces. Some scholars argue that while the Prophet's ﷺ heart and mind are protected from such influences, there is no proof that he could not be harmed in terms of his physical health.

The Holy Prophet ﷺ :

Some verses have been revealed to me that are unlike any that have come before: Sūrah al-Falaq and Sūrah al-Nās.

(Majmaʿ al-Bayān)

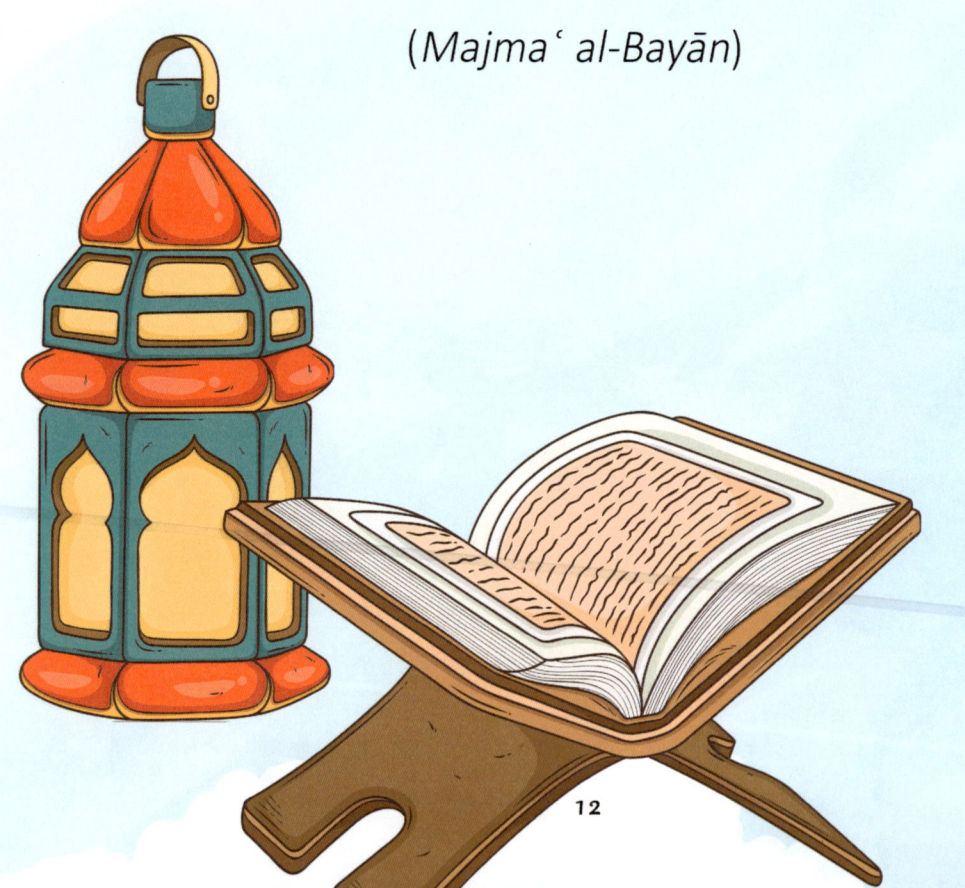

بِسْمِ اللَّهِ الرَّحْمَٰنِ الرَّحِيمِ

Bismillāhir Raḥmānir Raḥīm

In the Name of Allah, The Most Gracious,
The Most Merciful.

قُلْ أَعُوذُ بِرَبِّ الْفَلَقِ

Qul a-ūdhu bi-rabbil falaq

Say: I seek protection with the Lord of the Daybreak.

The word *Falaq* (فَلَق) means to split or separate. For example, when day breaks and splits away from the night, we call it *Falaq*.

This idea of splitting can be seen in many things, such as plants splitting from seeds, springs splitting from the earth and rain splitting apart from the clouds.

Ultimately, it is Allah ﷻ who splits darkness from evil, bringing forth light and guidance.

مِن شَرِّ مَا خَلَقَ

Min sharri mā khalaq

From the evil of which He has created.

Allah ﷻ tells us that everything He creates has a good purpose. When we ask for protection from evil, we're talking about things that might seem harmful to us.

For example, earthquakes and volcanoes help balance the earth, or a snake's venom protects it from danger. Even though these things have a good role in creation, they can sometimes harm us, which is why we see them as evil.

In this verse, we are asking Allah ﷻ to protect us from these potential harms.

وَمِن شَرِّ غَاسِقٍ إِذَا وَقَبَ

Wa min sharri ghāsiqin idhā waqab

And from the evil of the darkness when it comes.

Scary and harmful creatures, robbers and other dangers often come out at night to cause harm. This can also refer to spiritual darkness—a time when you're lost in the world, unsure and in need of guidance.

In this verse, we ask Allah ﷻ to protect us not only from physical dangers but also from the spiritual darkness that can leave us feeling lost.

وَمِن شَرِّ النَّفَّاثَاتِ فِي الْعُقَدِ

Wa min sharrin naffā-thāti fil 'uqad

And from the evil of those who blow on knots.

Who are the evil ones who blow on knots?

This refers to witches or magicians who bind their spells by tying knots and blowing on them to invoke harm.

Another interpretation suggests that these evil ones could symbolise people who whisper harmful words, causing others to doubt themselves. By doing so, they loosen the knots in their hearts, making them vulnerable and manipulating them as though they were under a magic spell.

وَمِن شَرِّ حَاسِدٍ إِذَا حَسَدَ

Wa min sharri ḥāsidin idhā ḥasad

And from the evil of the envious (ones) when they envy.

Envy means feeling upset or resentful because someone else has something you wish to have. It's not just wanting what they have, but also wishing that it be taken away from them.

Envious people often hold grudges and become consumed by anger.

In Islam, envy is considered one of the major sins because it can lead to harm and negativity towards others.

From the beginning of this *Sūrah*, we ask Allah ﷺ for help and protection from four specific types of evil:

1. All harmful things that we see as evil.

2. The dangers that come with the darkness of the night.

3. The evil of those who blow knots and try to weaken our faith with temptations and whispers.

4. The harm caused by those who are envious.

We seek protection from Allah ﷺ, as He is *'Rabbil Falaq'* (رَبِّ الْفَلَقِ), the Lord who splits the evil and darkness, bringing light and guidance.

Through this, we acknowledge that true safety, guidance and protection come from Allah ﷻ alone, who controls everything in creation.

He is the only One who can protect us from both visible dangers and hidden harms.

Glossary

Falaq — Split

Qiblah — Direction of the Kaʻbah

Rabb — Nurturer

Sūrah — Chapter

Sūrah al-Falaq — Chapter of the Daybreak

Sūrah al-Nās — Chapter of the People

Credit

All praise belongs to Allah, the All Merciful towards all existents, the Kindest towards believers. He Who has given us enough patience and courage to complete this book.

Islamic Lessons Made Easy would like to thank all those involved in this project for their hard work and commitment.

CREATOR
Abbas Ibrahim

EDITORS
Kawthar Ibrahim
Sheikh Dr Zaid Alsalami

Allahumma ṣalli ʿala Muḥammadi(n)w wa āli Muḥammad
O Allah, (please do) bless Muḥammad and the Household of Muḥammad

Contact: admin@islamiclessonsmadeeasy.com.au

Visit us:
Facebook.com/islamiclessonsmadeeasy
Youtube.com/islamiclessonsmadeeasy
Instagram.com/islamic_lessons_me
Islamiclessonsmadeeasy.com.au
Ilme.net.au

www.ingramcontent.com/pod-product-compliance
Lightning Source LLC
Chambersburg PA
CBRC091203070526
44583CB00008B/184